TERMINAL MORAINE

*For Karen —
fellow Banff-ite!*

TERMINAL MORAINE

all the best,

IAN LETOURNEAU

Edited by
Kent Bruyneel

thistledown press

Thistledown Press Ltd.
633 Main Street
Saskatoon, Saskatchewan, S7H 0J8
www.thistledownpress.com

Library and Archives Canada Cataloguing in Publication
LeTourneau, Ian, 1975-
Terminal moraine / Ian LeTourneau.
Poems.
ISBN 978-1-897235-53-9
I. Title.
PS8623.E9276T47 2008   C811'.54   C2008-904526-2

Publisher Cataloging-in-Publication Data (U.S)
(Library of Congress Standards)
LeTourneau, Ian.
Terminal moraine / Ian LeTourneau.
[64] p. : cm.
Summary: A collection of poems that assemble a past we pretend not to remember, a future we try not to remember, and a present we cannot escape.
ISBN: 978-1-897235-53-9 (pbk.)
1. Canadian poetry — 21st century. I. Title.
811.6 dc22 PS3612.E8Te   2008

Cover photograph (detail) by Taylor Leedahl
Cover and book design by Jackie Forrie
Printed and bound in Canada

10 9 8 7 6 5 4 3 2 1

Thistledown Press gratefully acknowledges the financial assistance of the Canada Council for the Arts, the Saskatchewan Arts Board, and the Government of Canada through the Book Publishing Industry Development Program for its publishing program.

ACKNOWLEDGEMENTS

Thanks to the editors of the following magazines where some of these poems first surfaced, often in earlier incarnations: *Arc*, *The Antigonish Review*, *Event*, *The Fiddlehead*, *Legacy*, *The Green Stone Mountain Review*, and *The Malahat Review*.

Thanks to Gaspereau Press, publishers of *Defining Range*, a limited edition chapbook of poems in the Devil's Whim chapbook series.

Thanks to the following publishers of the anthologies where some of these poems have appeared: *Alberta Anthology 2005* (Red Deer Press), *Talk that Mountain Down* (littlefishcartpress), *Alberta Anthology 2006* (Frontenac House), *Writing the Land* (House of Blue Skies), and *Gaspereau Gladiator Volume 1* (Gaspereau Press).

Thanks to The New Brunswick Arts Board, the Canada Council for the Arts, The Banff Centre and the Alberta Foundation for the Arts for financial assistance while working on this collection.

Thanks to the many editors who have offered their advice along the way, especially my Thistledown editor, Kent Bruyneel. Special thanks also to Ross Leckie, Don McKay, Stan Dragland, Marilyn Bowering, and Brian Bartlett. The Ice House gang in Fredericton was always supportive and helpful.

Thanks to everyone at Thistledown Press.

Thanks to my friends and family.

This book is for my son Wyatt.

Contents

I: Convergence Zones

10 A Cubist View of the Saint John River

11 Ordinary Day at the Beach

12 Last Moment of Childhood

13 Turtle

14 Identification

15 Witch's Broom

16 Alaska Highway

17 Winter Landscape, Promising: Mannville, Alberta

18 Bears

19 Mosquito

20 Short Song of Despair

21 The Robin

22 Silver

23 The Wineglass

24 Bath

II: Defining Range

26 Departure

27 Unidentified Birds

28 Winter Landscape, Promising:
   Fredericton, New Brunswick

29 Tearing Down an Old Barn

30 Squid Simulacrum

31 Between Sea and Sky

32 Migration

33 Song for the Mountain Crocus, Late Spring 2005

34 Eating Ice Cream

35 Dragonfly: A Triolet

36 Mushroom

37 Paradelle

38 Fireplace

39 Aurora Chorus

40 Trans-Canada, Northern Ontario

41 Embraceable You

42 · Noticed

43 Travertine

44 Field Guide Maps (Map 137, Sanderling)

III: TERMINAL MORAINE

46 Nickel Tailings #31, Sudbury, Ontario

47 Terminal Moraine

48 Carrara Marble Quarries #25, Carrara, Italy

49 Study: Mountain Air

50 Vision of My Old Age from a Shadow in a Photograph

51 Kinds of Apple #9 (Golden Delicious)

52 Oil Fields #24. Oil Sands, Fort McMurray, Alberta

53 Wind Farm

54 Tank

55 Sleep

56 Night

57 Bicycle

58 Pump Jacks

59 Shipbreaking #13, Chittagong, Bangladesh

60 The Dodo

61 Bow River Valley

62 Song for the Muskox

The mind was an emanation of the brain, just as bile was an excretion of the liver — something purely physical in character; while the soul, as far as such a term could be admitted, was the total effect of all the hereditary and personal functionings of the mind. But he also recognized that knowledge never stayed still, and that today's certainties might become tomorrow's superstitions. Therefore, the intellectual duty to continue looking never ceased.

— Julian Barnes, *Arthur & George*

. . . everything points to non-existence except existence.

— Robert Lowell, *History*

I: Convergence Zones

I know nothing that can give a better notion of infinity and eternity than the being upon the sea in a little vessel without anything in sight but yourself within the whole hemisphere.

— from *The Tangier Papers of Samuel Pepys*

A Cubist View of the Saint John River

Stasis. This morning, the concrete piers
of the old train bridge transform the river

into a factory of ice:
a Duchamp, nude and mechanical.

Gliding over the current,
the river's thin integument cracks.

Fracture, movement. A roiling dislocation,
a river hymnary. Fissures

and comings-apart vault morning light,
the impression of a conveyor belt.

Packed tight after separation,
the joints and hinges of ice allow ·

the river to roll back on itself
endlessly, but still move slowly forward.

A great peregrination headed out to merge
with the bay, assume

the identity of ocean. We can't control
the flow, our stories liquifying

into moments, a synthesis of now
and then. Instinctive, the river follows

its own meandering path.
The floating ice surrenders.

Ordinary Day at the Beach

After swimming, the water dried
to salt on my skin. The tide reversed,
revealed a pebbled coast,
and a large barnacle-encrusted rock.
Barnacles: I broke the seal of suction holding
them in place, admiring their glazed,
mottled shells. I was transfixed
by the shy antennaed life moving
within the whorl of its world.
I tried to coax the tiny creature
to its threshold, but it retreated each time
my fingers got too close. The sun
baked my footprints in the sand.

But then the tide began its slow
reclamation of the beach, climbing
up the slope to where I stood, handling
the shells in my hands like new words,
half-submerged in new meaning.
Not knowing what to do with them,
I left them on the sand next
to their rocky universe, heeding the call
for home. I went heavy with the sad
and monstrous knowledge that the power
I used to pluck them from their rock equaled
neither my power to restore
nor my newfound desire to redeem.

Last Moment of Childhood

I stood on the threshold
between the kitchen and living room.
The phone rang. The correspondent
on the evening news was reporting live.
Three simultaneous realities
were unfolding at once.

It was like leaving the stage
of an Elizabethan play and entering
a crowded restaurant. The world
was no longer filled with people rehearsing
for my arrival. And I kept
that last minute of childhood to myself.

Turtle
(for John Lofranco)

When I say that I withdraw from the world,
I don't mean with the wisdom of the turtle
who retreats between carapace and plastron,

avoiding confrontation. I'm not referring
to the lost years when the young venture
from their home beach to convergence zones

before returning to the self-same coast.
Where do they go? There is modesty
(if not certitude) in this enigmatic

withdrawal. One rite of passage in a long list
of passages. A projection of the inborn, perhaps,
though I like to believe differently.

There is no place for us to retreat
except to the sea of ideas, and daily
the mind is trawling up more and more turtles

in its by-catch. It should be remarkable
to hold the prehistoric, breathing, in your hands.

Identification

O barn cat *extremis*, o loner of the forests,
like many things in life, the glimpse
was unexpected, over as it was happening,
briefer than your tail, like a pencil
that doesn't fit behind the ear, whose grasp
on language is slipping. The field guide
says I should consider myself lucky
to have seen you at all. Swaggering
across Highway 2, tufted ears, oversized paws,
thick tawny fur, followed by the stump of tail.
Then the name arrives like sudden rain: *Lynx*.
Later, I read how your life depends, literally,
on snowshoe hare, how your population
closely tracks its life-cycles. O lynx, remind
me again about the possible renewal
of even an ordinary stretch of road.

Witch's Broom

An extension of spruce: a bristly
network of needles on twisted twigs.
Like many growths, it's awkward,

distorted. A nest-like coagulation
of air. Fungal magic. And I arrived
late for the premiere, the great unveiling —

was it a wave of branch? uncloaked
by night? *Chrysomyxa arctostaphyli.*
Though parasitic, it doesn't harm the tree.

Misshapen, it stands out, mistaken
for a squirrel's home, or like one of many
things we take for granted.

Alaska Highway

Out of fog — I slam on the brakes — dark and wooly shapes
appear. Bison, from the last free-range herd. Humped shoulders.
Immense horned heads fixed forward on their annual migration.
Fall is coming, or (this far north) here. These bison move
smoothly, the way a canoeist yields to the current. One looks my
way. I look back. The world

re-orders itself. The bison
lumber on. I watch.

The seatbelt, secure
on my shoulder and hip,
converts the car into a cage.

I can't undo anything.
I'll drive the rest of this road,
get somewhere I called home.

Winter Landscape, Promising: Mannville, Alberta

Pine siskins don't seem to mind early snow,
or that prairie leaves mostly turn pale gold.
Although there's no way to absolutely know,
I'd hazard that this lack of colour — a bold
oversimplification — is not about withholding.
It's a clarity of purpose: every detail, including
death, is observed here. Before the prairie
was settled, these birds chattered
only for the wind, which steadily
reshaped the order of leaves. What mattered?
Only seed and wind and rain and snow,
for which the siskins prepare with cursive flight,
dropping from higher branches to ones below.
They wait for winter to gather in the night.

Bears

Last summer, we hiked up the Coal Lake Road
near Whitehorse. After two hours we reached
tree line, where the trail leveled out.
An acrid musk thickened the air in our throats.

Up ahead, something black loomed from behind
some scrub birch and strolled across the path
toward a lone stunted fir. Things suddenly
acquired an unexpected aura; words

were no longer needed. We started
back, eager to gather the fragments
of our shattered language at the trailhead,
to encounter another human face,

to redefine fir and rocks, as a young bear must,
after being chased into the woods,
faced with first emptiness.

Mosquito

Sitting on a patio, a humid summer night,
we agreed that mosquitoes had intentions.

You applied some lip gloss: clear, fragrant,
all-natural. So much like the sheen of human sweat,

of bare arms, legs.

There's something about the mosquitoes' persistence,
you said. We talked into the dark hours, swatting.

Around us, torches of perfumed fire. No matter how often
we brushed away their desire for flesh, one after another,

the mosquitoes descended.

Short Song of Despair

On my bike, I sail down the hill towards
water. Gravel crunches like candles.

There is a resonance here of memory's
tuning fork, intoning the timbre of your

voice: a nubile hiss of waves rolling in,
rolling out, attempting with their contortions

an uneasy balance. The sun eases
into the hill's crenellations, into the river —

simple things matter: your words,
for instance, once common as pigeons.

The Robin

Yesterday, while we were reading Werther
in the woods, we heard a robin singing
in the branches and I held your hands,
your white hands, and spoke to you of love.
But you weren't listening to me,
my words steeped in youthful pretension.

Suddenly, you rose and ran through the myrtle,
and you called to me, "Look," and I came.
And here was the robin, this poor bird
of spring, fallen from the leaves, moonstruck.
It was young, and wounded, and dying.
And you, moved by its suffering, cried.
And I stared at the empty sky and thought,
the robin and my love have both died.

> — translated from the French,
> Emile Nelligan's "Le Robin des Bois"

Silver

I want to say all is silver, but it's not; it's only
the uppermost branches of these elms that gleam

with a silvered varnish of ice, blending into a sky
absent of blue. Notice how the sun layers

a single uneven coat over the bareness;
how it copies the twisted paths branches take.

This state is elemental. Your car, like the elms,
is covered with the brittle armour of the ice pellets

that fell last night, and briefly glints in the morning sun.
With the car brush, you scrape away the shell,

reveal your reflection in the car window.
In one glance, you see the sun, the silvered branches,

and yourself — unmistakable — in the curving middle.
As you move, you swear you melt into sky.

The Wineglass
(for Sherry Coffey)

The vanished meal lingers in the scents of garlic,
tarragon. And your bottom lip smudged along the rim of

this wineglass — a printing so fine it may have
been left by the grazing of a feather tip. This smear

is supple, suggests ripe tomatoes, plum. Or a slice
of moon emerging from the river. This stubborn

blushing. This is artifact — the glass already warping
memory: as though the curving grains of the oak table,

the chair you sat in, and the painting of flowers
on the wall reveal potential. There is yet no

correlation between the world as it is and the world
behind the glass, tugged into deliquescence.

This smear pulls me forward, says nothing
but is wholly you, vertiginous: a stain waiting to lift

off into an explanation of plumage.

Bath

Glasses clang together as we slide
stacks of dirty dishes from last night
aside to give you a bath in the sink.
You're five weeks old now, faraway
from the day you'll leave home,
as every child does.

The roasting pan is slick with olive oil
and dappled with dried herbs,
the rosemary still fragrant. The cutlery
is crusted with particles of food.
These chores will never go away.

Yet one day you will. They will tell you history
repeats itself but, in fact, we repeat history,
just as you repeat the few syllables
you've stumbled upon over and over,
trying to perfect them. History doesn't
chronicle the mundane, like dishes,
or your joy, as you churn water with your legs.
Your gleeful syllables splashing on our ears.

II: Defining Range

*For as the eyes of bats are to the blaze of day, so
is the reason in our soul to the things which are by
nature most evident of all.*

— Aristotle, *Metaphysics*.

Departure
(for Holly Luhning)

Perhaps, to a red-winged blackbird, the wind
is a weigh station, a last survey of dandelions,
cinnamon ferns, before migration.

Reflexes become initials scraped on birch
bark, their taste hints of chokecherry.
If there is a grace to departing, it is this:

to be at ease with shifting landscapes,
for under the surface of an entire sand dune,
the roots and rhizomes of marram grass

connect. Thousands of years have shaped
the sand into Persian script. But there is an order
to loss: clouds drift by as they have to,

on their way somewhere important, or just
passing through this marmoreal blue. The sky
twitches here and there with flight, signifying,

simply, an openness, or what's possible.

Unidentified Birds

I'm watching birds this morning that I think
are black and white warblers, who, if indeed
turn out to be black and white warblers, then
have traveled great distances to reach
the poplar and spruce in the backyard.
But I'm uncertain. They constantly escape
the two rings of my binoculars' vision.
Like those nephews or nieces who fidget
out of photographs at weddings
or family reunions, they're beyond my control.

Much like you and your growth, your heart
beating twice as fast as mine. The tiny bones
of your fingers, which you can bend now,
are the first indication of your will.
One day you'll use those same fingers, point
at things I will help you name,
perhaps even these unidentified birds.

Though I enjoy watching their manic
branch-hopping before they leave, I could
be wrong about everything. Perhaps this blur
of wings is a lesson in humility.
Every year these birds will return.
There's so much beauty in the world, son;
prepare to be overwhelmed.

Winter Landscape, Promising:
Fredericton, New Brunswick

Vernal equinox, misplaced: the first snowfall
melting; paint again seeps up through winter's
temporary canvas, as if repetition was more than

repetition: a dog shaking rain off matted fur.
The skeletal branches of weathered elms
seem like seasonal sequelae in the vacuum

of sun. At this time of year the sky blooms
earlier each night: purple scars wheedled
from blue. It's only when we ask why

the palette appears duller after each storm
we realize the constant redefining,
the blending into white.

Each winter is different,
yet we rummage for comparisons.

Tearing Down an Old Barn

We can only reclaim so much barn board
for furniture or to frame a painting
with an antique touch. It's not as easy

as it seems, this coming-apart, this slow
fragmentation of the barn, whose wood
has weathered grey. Better to reclaim

before rot. Wedge the crowbar gently
at the top of each plank and coax
the rusted nail from its home. The wood

will groan as you pry each board
from its crossbeam. Each piece a harmony
of grains flowing around the knots, nails

singing an elegy for remembered seasons.
A hint of green visible through barn ribs.

Squid Simulacrum

In ink, the squid projects
a near-perfect replica of itself
when threatened, a mirror-

warped counterfeit,
so that it can sluice through
the ocean's depths like a red dart.

It has other ways to defend itself,
of course: many whales
are underwater art galleries,

great, gliding exhibits
of tattooed sucker rings
in overlapping circular patterns.

But nothing is as urgent as
the re-creation of itself,
how in one blot the squid

depicts squidkind, its tentacled
essence almost perfectly replicated
down to fin, funnel and mantle.

So accurate that even those creatures
who would do it harm are charmed
by the brief, enchanting shapes

ink forms. How its inky vocabulary
simulates
the substance of a soul.

Between Sea and Sky

Open water. A sail pregnant with wind
glides across the mirror of the sea. What lies
beneath is unfathomable. Instead, we find
around us, if we search, a compromise

of the horizon, vice-gripped between decisions
of sea and sky. This wedge is no casual synthesis;
the waves offer their revision.
No straight lines actually exist.

The sun, having just trespassed across the line,
for instance, is the embryo of morning,

unsure of night or day. Take that, combined
with human history, the constant rebirthing

of war, and our dreams, once so fixed, hovering
like this horizon, remain undefined.

Migration

At first a few honks, as audible
as the opening bars of minimalist jazz.
We might question its musicality.
But then approaching like a dark cloud,
the syncopated honks of the flock
increase, as each takes the turn to lead
the group. Deafening, the noise of lane
after lane of geese, the improvised melody
of an ordered highway in the sky.

Song for the Mountain Crocus, Late Spring 2005

When I saw my first mountain crocus —
slight lavender petals emerging from the side

of the trail — I thought of Donne
as he rode westward in 1613, his soul bent

towards home. There is a remarkable flexibility
to the soul, a firstling of sorts, like

this flower, which we also call *pasque*,
Easter, with its undertow of death and resurrection.

New life. Remember last Easter when we had
a house full of family, a rite of passage

to have guests in *our* home. Your nieces,
who sang the unbroken melodies of childhood,

opened unknown spaces within me like
this crocus cracking open ground. Ready

to hear the untuned music of family and
hum along to its possibilities.

Eating Ice Cream

In the cradle of the bowl of blueberries
mixed with vanilla ice cream I have

finished eating, a Rorschach test appears.
Colours intermingle, blue and white

becoming various shades of red. Mountains
with a setting sun, you say; I say

decomposing butterflies, transmogrified
into questions for which we crave answers,

a sense that the fluttering anticipation
of children foregrounds other desires.

Not that we lack answers or choice —
after all, they're smeared across the bottom

of this bowl. Outside, the sky is a nursery
of stars, of which our knowledge remains inexact.

Dragonfly: A Triolet

Lifeless, fused to the grill of the car,
but shining in its own peculiar way
like a piece of broken jewelry.

Lifeless, fused to the grill of the car.
I notice the wing first, its bent angle,
pinned there in such an unnatural way.

Lifeless, fused to the grill of the car,
but shining in its own peculiar way.

Mushroom

Each morning, we walk on a paved path.
The sun brightly crests the valley,
more resilient than the day before.

Benches mark our progress.
Yesterday, a wild mushroom had pushed
through the edge of the black asphalt.

The asphalt crumbled so easily, leaving
a dark heap of clay and dirt and pave
and mushroom. Long after the vegetable

matter decays, there will be a small crater
here — a relic, an impact — at least until
the spot is patched, made orderly again.

Paradelle

I remember there was a melody to your voice.
I remember there was a melody to your voice.
You left its unbroken song to linger in my head.
You left its unbroken song to linger in my head.
A song in my head. Its voice was unbroken. You
linger there. I remember your melody left. To.

Soon the melody changed and I was alone.
Soon the melody changed and I was alone.
I walked along the river to watch its ceaseless flow.
I walked along the river to watch its ceaseless flow.
Ceaseless, the river soon walked alone. I was changed.
And I watch its melody flow along. To the.

In the winter the river darkened and stilled.
In the winter the river darkened and stilled.
The birds flew away emptying the sky of your voice.
The birds flew away emptying the sky of your voice.
Your voice stilled the darkened sky. And in the winter
the emptying river of birds flew away. The.

Your winter birds remember the ceaseless melody
The melody of a darkened sky changed in my head.
The river left its song alone and walked away to you.
To you. The flow stilled and I was emptying
of voice. Its voice was in there. Soon I flew along.
I linger to watch the river. The unbroken.

Fireplace

O let's praise the combustible creature
of the fireplace. The fireproof masonry
of the sleek body, a column of scaly

brickwork that descends from the flue's
communion with sky. The clipped wings,
and the recessed place of fire, the hearth

where the inglenook of its jaw lies open
to receive offerings of ritual logs,
crumpled newsprint. Where, communally,

we sit enthralled by the downdrafts of warm
breath, currents that extinguish our cold comfort.
And the mantelpiece of its forehead, the bone

pate where pictures of loved ones stand ominously
framed, in reverence to the embers of coal-
like residue, the ash that once was dragon's soul.

Aurora Chorus

Heard melodies are sweet, but those unheard
Are sweeter . . .
                    — John Keats, "Ode on a Grecian Urn"

But now that we can hear those notes,
the sweetness is lost.
We've come from nightingales to this:

an unanswerable telephone call; an
otherworldly scritching
and popping like the space between songs on

a vinyl recording where the cello is a ghost
whistling. White noise
has never been so colourful. And it *is* noise:

an unordered musical loop half-way through
its progression.
The crackling anthem of silence.

Trans-Canada, Northern Ontario

Wipers swipe at oncoming headlights
and become Van Gogh star swirls
from the fog and rain. The swamps

and winding, rocky hills on the coast
of Lake Superior are thick with moose
ready to merge with traffic. Wind

shakes the car. Vehicles pass, creating
cataracts on the windshield, leaving
the eyes only seconds to readjust.

Then more supernovae and imaginary moose,
their shaggy outlines in every shadow.
Night itself becomes animal intention.

Embraceable You
(after Charlie Parker)

The notes embraced and freed
so that they return to the roost of the horn
to be shuffled out again. Desire
is ignited and abolished from

that first note, a small rock released
from a high hill, gathering
others to itself as a magnet
would, until the coda

of thundering debris subsides
into the nothing that replaces silence.

Noticed
(*for Stan Dragland*)

We may not have noticed after ten hours
of hiking, looking up mostly, vistas
of blue. We may not have noticed
if it weren't for this picture, taken by a friend,
who stopped, and because some happenstance thing
like light struck him, snapped it.
Only ten square feet of earth, framed,
where roots of spruce and pine overlap,
connecting rows of trees in a vast disorderly
network, worn from the slow workings
of weather and hiking boots. Needles, moss,
twigs sifted and shifted on top.

There must be a will of seed, having blown
this way, settled on this order, having frisked
for fertile soil in the sub-alpine air.

Though we all stopped to look at the first flowers
of the year, glacier lilies nodding
their drooping yellow heads,
we passed right by the interlocking sturdiness
of these trees. And because it was
ordinary, went unnoticed.

Travertine
(Johnson's Canyon, Banff National Park)

When we saw the copulating squirrels, we cringed
for a father's awkwardness as his daughter
laughed wildly. On that same hike,

I marvelled at a travertine drape, how its paradox
is enviable: half rock, half living thing.
Washed over by an unbroken continuity

of calcium-rich water for thousands of years,
organism has fused with rock — algae and limestone.

And how this handful of natural impurities,
ordered in a chemical syntax, forms such things.

Like the daughter's laugh, halfway
between living thing and monument.

Field Guide Maps (Map 137, Sanderling)
(for Don McKay)

These maps outline alternate continents, unique
to each species of bird, defining range in a few
broad strokes of colour. Fantastic Beringias.
Stills of northern lights. Blobs. For instance,
the splotch of pink high in the arctic islands
to denote the Sanderling's breeding grounds.
And the blue (a rough idea of winter home)
specks the coast from the Aleutians through
the Inside Passage to Vancouver Island,
where home thickens into a line that curves
southward, tracing around the hip thrust of America.
But this is, of course, only gesture, a plot line
for the story behind flight. Common sense
(that insidious birder) is never far off:
"a Marsh Wren must have a marsh,
a Meadowlark a meadow." We observe
that Sanderlings prefer tideflats, shore
lines, to playfully chase the waves going out to sea.

These shapes could also be of receding continents,
shortening, and distinct, like the song
of the Sanderling. *Quit. Quit.* As if its song,
after a long migration, is jetlagged.
As if the bird's only desire is to sleep,
but it stays awake. Stares
at the retreating waves,
looking for reason.

III: Terminal Moraine

That great god

Tell him

*That we who follow you invented
forgiveness*

And forgive nothing

— W. S. Merwin, "For
a Coming Extinction"

Nickel Tailings #31, Sudbury, Ontario
(after a photograph by Edward Burtynsky)

Every indication is of natural disaster,
a river of thick orange carving its way
through a landscape of charred grass,

rock and earth — the endnotes of industry:

cropless fields,

disgorged creeks,

treeless horizon.

Terminal Moraine
(for the glaciers of the Canadian Rockies)

According to scientists, the glaciers
are receding at a speed incompatible
with the seasons, leaving piles of rock
in their wake. Terminal moraine: incredible

ridges of debris. It's no mistake. The fate
of this icy water, blue-green from glacial till,
is sealed. It's melting at constant rates
and will until the rushing water stills.

These dwindling masses of ice that connect
us to the past will be gone. The carving
of canyons will be left unfinished.

For now a few pine grow between fists
of rock, fed by the vanishing ice.
The date-markers inch steadily backward.

Carrara Marble Quarries #25, Carrara, Italy
(after a photograph by Edward Burtynsky)

Looking down:

inverted architecture, cubes of absence, or rather,
absence cubed.

Squiggles of detonating wire and rope vein
the white floor: automatic writing. Elsewhere,

the blocks are stacked into skyscrapers
or hacked into sublime things like *Cupid and Psyche*.
In Canova's version, Psyche lies on
a slope of marble, the very material from
which she is made, head extended back
in anticipation of a kiss from Cupid.
The moment is charged, explosive.
Cupid's wings are open, his forearm
cradles her breasts. This is before she sees
her new husband, before everything goes
bad.

Study: Mountain Air

The air is all pine needles
and lichen, which is to say,
scented philosophy,
stretched and purposeful,
which is to say, objective,
it ripens your cheeks.

The air is ritual, addictive,
which is to say, it swallows
mountains and rivers,
it is an ode to itself, which is
to say, an improviser, a magpie
chasing squirrels from tree to tree.

The air holds every line ever written,
which is to say, it is composed.
Your last word. Your eulogy.

Vision of My Old Age from a Shadow in a Photograph

Foreshadowing. An omen, perhaps, of what's to come.
A forecast of old age. There we are, just yesterday,
on top of Marten Mountain. Lesser Slave Lake
behind us to the west. You stand in the light
next to me and I partially eclipse the sun
as it tries to find your yellow shirt.
A stooped silhouette across
your chest. My profile
advanced half a century,
the firm line of my jaw loosened,
my glasses exaggerated, chin rounded
like these foothills that extend, undulating, to the flatline of the
    prairie.

Kinds of Apple #9 (Golden Delicious)

Rolling it slowly, I munch the golden
apple. By the time I meet the script
of my teeth's initial puncture

the exposed flesh is coppered
as if air had stirred mineral into
memory and the apple, unable

to resist, unveiled its stippled,
fibrous core. My thumb and forefinger
remain sticky with apple. Fragrance

at the apex of its sweetness.
This is conversion propelled by
hunger — convex to concave — where

the apple's perfect globe gives way
to the hourglass of appetite.

Oil Fields #24. Oil Sands, Fort McMurray, Alberta
(after a photograph by Edward Burtynsky)

You might think *badlands* at first,
but this landscape has been overturned,
sapped. Earth itself industrialized,
under revision.

This might be its final form, sandy
residuum, littered with the jargon of
lease agreements: reclamation, self-sustaining,
production. It frightens me sometimes
how these great machinations gnash on.
How the landscape can be mutated like this or
language: armamentarium to Armageddon.

One bulldozer, off-centred, signifies
I suppose, that our journey is industrial,
that this, last century's horizon, merges
with the future's receding green. The sky,
though light and wispy with clouds,
is the steady back beat of the blues.

Wind Farm

"Every revolution is about power."
— *Canadian Wind Energy Association* pamphlet

Wind becomes visible, jammed
through the propellers of each turbine.
Bringer of weather, most

sustainable conversation piece, it concentrates
on direction, which is mostly intuitive.
One might think there are limits to imagination

and have it confirmed when a bird (any songbird
will do) crashes into the weaponization
of air. *The wind bloweth where it listeth,*

but it must also disclose the essential component
of flight, namely lift — an interception
that churns air into energy, bending *where it goeth.*

O lubricant of society, o invisible possibilities.

Tank
(*Cambrai, November 1917*)

At first "landships" — to suggest an extension
of the navy. Then "tanks" — a nickname to hide
from German intelligence. Great temblors,
rumbling onto the Cambrai battlefield,
achieving speeds of three and half miles per hour.

Mechanical hardbacked beetles crawling
across no man's land, transforming the landscape
into denationalized uniformity: saplings, shells,
barbed wire, corpses. The whir

and steady rotation of caterpillar tracks
emerges from the cocoon of silence,
rumbling into an iron metamorphosis.

Sleep

She is asleep in front of the television set,
clutching the remote control. Utterly asleep.
I lift her, limbs dangling, into my arms to get
her off to bed, carefully, hoping she keeps
the safety of her dreams craddled in her head.
I hum her favourite lullaby — a little sound
at first — till we reach the side of her bed.
Turning the covers back, I lay her down.

Time collapses. An image resurfaces
from months ago: the coverage of war,
from the rubble of a building, a man is
carrying the body of a child. The jar
at first unsettles. Looking down, I see the life-
less body of that child. Closer, I see the life.

Night

Night
The silence of night
Surrounds me
Like a strong undertow.

I rest on the mute, green seafloor
I can hear my heart
Which flares and dims
Like a lighthouse.

Faint rhythm
Secret code
I won't solve any mysteries.

At each sweep of the beam
I close my eyes
For the remainder of night
Perpetual silence
Where I've sunk.

— translated from the French,
Anne Hébert's "La Nuit"

Bicycle

or bike. Until you became preoccupied
with distance, velocity, you remained a sketch
by DaVinci (or one of his students). Then

Baron von Drais wanted to circle the royal gardens
faster: two wheels to add grace to human motion.
But you were wooden, inflexible, just an idea

of thoroughbred, a *Hobby Horse* we propelled
with our feet. Fifty years later, you rattled along
the cobbled streets of Europe, two pedals attached

to a larger-than-life front wheel. *Boneshaker. Velocopedes.*
But when pneumatic tires first divided ground from
iron, you truly took off. That initial flight —

shaky — but then a lift from blurry ground — grass
and trees mingled to one colour. The paradox of
transforming body into engine: those things

closest move fastest away. Imagination gets cogged,
pulleyed, chained. Gears shift, ideas circle, recycle.
In the depression, you were practical, earned

affectionate nicknames: *Cruiser, Clunker, Bomber.*
Now, exhaustless, sweat-fueled, you climb mountains,
weave through traffic, endlessly adapt.

Pump Jacks

The field was probably a flank of wheat
or flax until the replication of pump jacks
began. In eerie formations,

they infinitely regress into the folds
of prairie, black and red mosquitoes,
practicing their mechanized manoeuvres.

In the momentary hesitation of the cog
before the jack's proboscis dips down,
and again down, into the earth,

you imagine the blurred wringing of hands,
the drool of oil from the effortless labour.
Moveable, insatiable, endless.

Shipbreaking #13, Chittagong, Bangladesh
(after a photograph by Edward Burtynsky)

These ships have been decommissioned,
their hulls hulled. Great steel chunks topple,
compelled by torch and gravity.

In the background, more ships wait.

The insides are unconcealed,
walls already sliced in jagged sections,
carried away for scrap, intimate
like the set of a never-ending play:
something about time or its finitude.

There are no people.
Just ships and parts of ships.

And on the tentative ground,
footprints being reclaimed
by the soft muck.

The Dodo
(Extinct c. 1670)

> *"A sentence uttered makes a world appear*
> *Where all things happen as it says they do."*
> — W.H. Auden, "Words"

Yes, that's a solid argument. But consider
the Dodo, *Raphus cucullatus*, and the earliest
extant account in print, 1627. Sir Thomas Herbert
wrote of their "shape and rareness," with-
out irony. The Dodo stored nutmeg-sized stones
in its gizzard to crush food. The English fed
them for entertainment. "Nature's injurie"
of which Herbert so eloquently spoke
is that we'll never see the animation
of their eyes — "small and like to Diamonds"
— even though diamonds are everywhere.

Bow River Valley

The sun wobbles through the sky, flipped
each morning like a thick gold coin.
The toss is predictable — east to west.
We've named and numbered the days.

It's easy to recline into despair, prop our feet
up and let the slippers thud to the floor
like a large book, say, Gibbon's *Decline
and Fall of the Roman Empire*.

Why do I think of Rome's headless statues?
Must be these uncountable phalanxes
of pine converging upon the banks
of the river. In war, it was noble

to die for the empire, and then some: honour
lifted a soldier on top of a bier, wooden planks
and kindling set ablaze, allowing
the spirit to rise in columns of smoke.
Two gold coins resting on the eyes.

Song for the Muskox

Often in the reliquary of my imagination, a muskox stands
in tall grass, which blows in a tundra-stiffened wind.

It snorts through prehistoric nostrils. A robe of dark,
silver-flecked silk covers its flanks. Curved horns

point toward the tors and tussocks. The sky is the blue
of compacted ice. Gravelly eskers crenellate

the abundant nothingness. All the elements that form
the world — rock, water, life — are here. Red and arctic fox

print their tracks on white snow, as do caribou, moose, grizzly,
polar bear. Other muskoxen join, circle the mind

and life is suddenly unrecognizable. I am
Sir Walter Raleigh, condemned citizen, head facing

north on the execution block. I shout,
but the words transform into chamois. In the layers below

permafrost is unspoiled truth. *Bring it on*, I say,
there is gold in Guiana. Ice shelves crumble in the distance.